21st Century Junior Library

RESPONSIBILITY

by Lucia Raatma

CHERRY LAKE PUBLISHING * ANN ARBOR, MICHIGAN

Published in the United States of America by Cherry Lake Publishing
Ann Arbor, Michigan
www.cherrylakepublishing.com

Reading Adviser: Cecilia Minden-Cupp, PhD, Literacy Consultant

Photo Credits: Page 4, ©iStockphoto.com/Fertnig; page 6, ©Kuttig-People/Alamy; cover
and page 8, ©iStockphoto.com/video1; page 10, ©Vera Tomankova, used under license
from Shutterstock, Inc.; cover and page 12, ©Monkey Business Images, used under license from
Shutterstock, Inc.; page 14, ©Tetra Images/Alamy; page 16, ©Morgan Lane Photography, used
under license from Shutterstock, Inc.; cover an page 18, ©iStockphoto.com/ShaneKato; cover and
page 20, ©Juan Manuel Ordóñez, used under license from Shutterstock, Inc.

LIBRARY OF CONGRESS CATALOGING-IN-PUBLICATION DATA
Raatma, Lucia.
 Responsibility / by Lucia Raatma.
    p. cm. — (Character education)
 Includes index.
 ISBN-13: 978-1-60279-321-7
 ISBN-10: 1-60279-321-2
 1. Responsibility—Juvenile literature. I. Title.
 BJ1451.R23 2009
 179'.9—dc22   2008029290

*Cherry Lake Publishing would like to acknowledge the work of
The Partnership for 21st Century Skills.
Please visit* **www.21stcenturyskills.org** *for more information.*

CONTENTS

5 What Is Responsibility?

9 Being Responsible

15 Being Responsible in Your Community

22 Glossary

23 Find Out More

24 Index

24 About the Author

Helping with chores at home is one way to act responsibly.

What Is Responsibility?

"Thanks, Max! You're a big help." Max smiled when his mom said that. He had cleared the table and taken the garbage out. He had checked the chart in the kitchen. It was his turn to do these chores.

"You are so responsible," his mom continued.

Max felt good. He knew that he was doing his part.

What would you do if you broke a friend's toy?

When you are responsible, you are **reliable**. People can count on you. You do what you say you are going to do. You don't expect others to do your work.

Being responsible also means owning up to mistakes. You don't blame other people. If you break something, you **admit** it. If you forget to meet your friend after school, you apologize.

Do you ever help your parents make dinner? Helping prepare meals is just one way to show you are responsible.

Being Responsible

There are many ways to be responsible. You can do your chores at home. You can keep your room clean. You can help take care of your family's pets. You can help your parents make dinner.

Create!

Ask a parent to help you make a chore chart. List all of the chores you are responsible for each week. Check off the tasks as you finish them. That way, you won't forget anything.

Having pets is a big responsibility. They depend on you to take care of them.

Being responsible means thinking before you act. It means keeping in mind how your actions may affect others.

What if you forget to feed your pet rabbit? It will be hungry for the rest of the day. What if you forget to take out the garbage? It may overflow or attract insects.

Responsible students always try to do their best work.

There are many ways to be responsible at school. Being responsible means listening in class. It means finishing your **assignments** on time. It also means following the rules at school.

Ask Questions!

Are you confused about an assignment? Ask questions! Be sure you understand what you are supposed to do. Teachers will be happy to help you. Asking questions can help you do the best job you can on assignments.

Collecting items for people in need is one
way to be responsible.

Being Responsible in Your Community

Everyone plays a part in making the world a better place. You can be responsible by **volunteering**. Make volunteering a family event. Find something that is important to you and your parents. Then find out what you can do to help. Maybe you can all help collect clothing and food for people in need.

Responsible people help take care of Earth by recycling.

You can also be responsible by caring about your **environment**. A responsible person doesn't litter. A responsible person **recycles** bottles, cans, and paper.

Look!

Watch your favorite TV show. Are any of the characters acting responsibly? What are they doing that makes them responsible?

Have you ever helped your neighbors shovel snow
after a snowstorm?

Another way to be responsible is to help out in your neighborhood. Maybe you can work with your neighbors to clean up the local park. Or you can shovel snow for an older neighbor.

Can you think of some more ways
to be responsible?

When you are responsible, people know they can trust you. They know they can count on you to do what you have promised. Being responsible is good for you. It is also good for all the people around you!

Think!

Remember a time when you were not responsible. What happened and how did you feel? Then remember a time when you were very responsible. How did you feel then?

GLOSSARY

admit (ad-MIT) to agree that something is true; to confess to something

assignments (uh-SINE-muhnts) jobs that are given to certain people to do; homework given to you by a teacher is an assignment

environment (en-VYE-ruhn-muhnt) the world around you, including the land, sea, and air

recycles (ree-SYE-kuhlz) processes old items so they can be used to make new products

reliable (ri-LYE-uh-buhl) describing someone whom others can depend on and trust

volunteering (VOL-uhn-TIHR-ing) offering to do a job for no pay

FIND OUT MORE

BOOKS

Kroll, Virginia L. *Jason Takes Responsibility*. Morton Grove, IL: Albert Whitman & Company, 2005.

Suen, Anastasia. *Don't Forget: A Responsibility Story*. Edina, MN: Magic Wagon, 2008.

WEB SITES

PBS Kids—It's My Life: Pet Responsibilities
pbskids.org/itsmylife/family/pets/article3.html
Read more about what it takes to be a responsible pet owner

PBS Kids—Making Money: Responsibility
pbskids.org/itsmylife/money/making/article6.html
Learn about ways to be responsible when it comes to working and earning money

INDEX

A
actions, 11
admitting mistakes, 7
affects, 11
apologies, 7
assignments, 13

B
blame, 7

C
chores, 5, 9, 11

E
environment, 17

F
family, 5, 9, 15
forgetting, 7, 9, 11
friends, 7

L
listening, 13
littering, 17

M
mistakes, 7

N
neighborhood, 19

P
parents, 9, 15
promises, 21

Q
questions, 13

R
recycling, 17
reliability, 7
rules, 13

S
school, 13

T
teachers, 13
thinking, 11
trust, 21

V
volunteering, 15

ABOUT THE AUTHOR

Lucia Raatma has written dozens of books for young readers. They are about famous people, historical events, ways to stay safe, and other topics. She lives in Florida's Tampa Bay area with her husband and their two children.